Rolf Heimann's MEGA Mind•twisters

Watermill Press

First published in USA by Watermill Press, an imprint of Troll Associates, Inc.

Copyright © 1993 Rolf Heimann

Printed in USA

ISBN 0-8167-3393-7
10 9 8 7 6 5 4 3 2

Mind-twisting message

When I finish writing and illustrating a book like this, I feel exhausted. My mind is like jelly, my eyes are throbbing, and my brain feels like it has been washed, wrung out, and hung up to dry. And that is how I want *you* to feel when you have finished the last puzzle in this book!

You might think I'm being cruel, but if you can get through these puzzles and mazes with only one or two peeks at the solutions on page 29, then I know that you have taken your mind to the limit, and that it will be in first-class condition.

Good luck on your trek through Mega Mind-twisters.

Rolf Heimann

Absent-minded artist

Our artist in the clouds wanted to paint a picture that included all of his favorite objects, pictured on the opposite page. However, when he finished the painting he realized that he had left three out! *Can you see which objects are missing?*

◇2◇ **Baffling butterflies**

Butterflies are usually symmetrical (that means that the pattern on one wing is a mirror-reflection of the pattern on the other), but those that are not are prized by butterfly collectors as very rare. Two of the butterflies in this collection are not symmetrical. Which ones are they?

3 Strings attached

If you pull on the strings, the letters will slide into place. *What is the boy's name, and what is the dinosaur called?*

Look at these flowers! They're arranged just like the Southern Cross!

And there are 26 other arrangements like it.

4 Southern stars

The Southern Cross, or *Crux Australis*, is a prominent star constellation in the skies of the Southern Hemisphere. *Can you find all the objects in this picture that are arranged in the same way?*

5 ▷ Royal reflection

There is definitely something wrong with the King's magic mirror. Not less than twenty things are incorrectly reflected! *Can you spot them?*

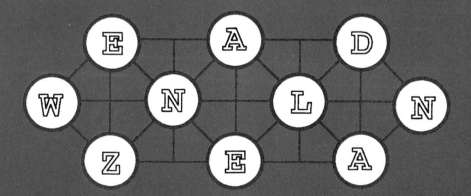

6 ▷ Country connection

The name of a country is hidden in this puzzle. Follow the lines from one letter to the next, but don't jump over any circles!

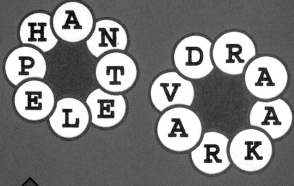

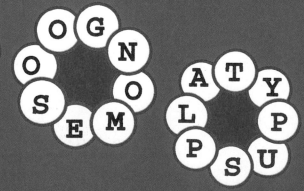

7 Around in circles

Reading either clockwise or counter-clockwise, these circles spell out the names of four animals.

Big Dipper baffler

Many other objects in this illustration have arranged themselves in the same pattern as the star constellation *Ursa Major*. For instance, look at the leaves on the tree! *How many similar arrangements are there?* (Clue: don't forget to turn the page upside-down).

9 Mind-twisting mass

Is the bridge strong enough for the children's pet dinosaur?

African safari

Only one of these African harbor cities will let our intrepid explorer reach the lion in the middle of the continent. Which city is it? Time limit: one minute!

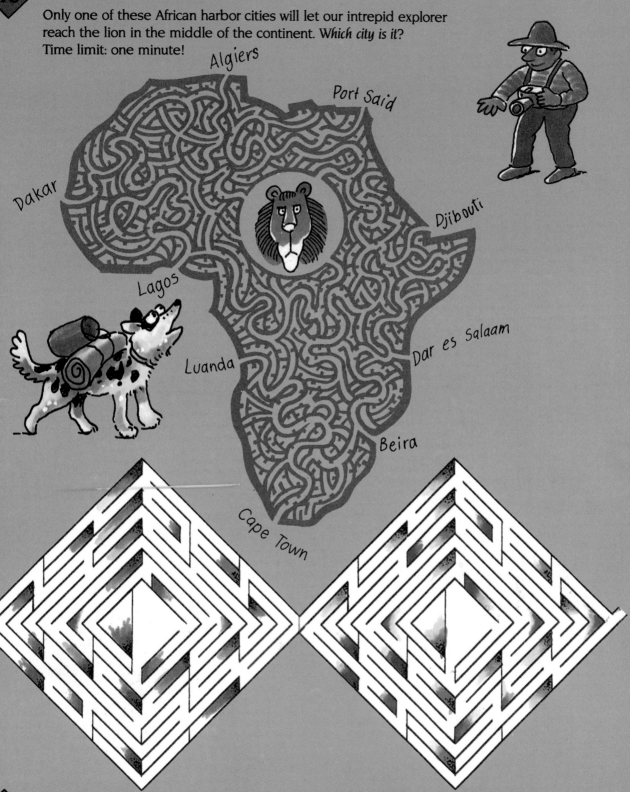

Double vision

Are you a quick learner? The path through the second diamond is exactly the same as the first, so you should get through it a lot faster. Time limit: first diamond: thirty seconds, second diamond: fifteen seconds.

Darwin

Cairns

Broome

Brisbane

Sydney

Fremantle

Adelaide

Melbourne

13 Aussie odyssey

Above is an outline of Australia, with the major coastal cities marked. *Where should our fearless explorer start his trek to find the gold?*

14 Blowing in the wind

Only one of the yachts around the compass points is the same as the one in the middle of the compass. *Which one is it?*

N

NW   NE

W   E

SW   SE

S

15 ▷ Island hopping

The names of seventeen of the world's better-known islands are hidden in this word puzzle and are marked on the world map below. The words in the puzzle may run in any direction, including diagonally.

E	C	O	R	S	I	C	A	R	F	N
T	M	H	O	N	S	H	U	J	I	E
M	A	D	A	G	A	S	C	A	R	W
O	W	S	U	R	P	Y	C	M	E	F
E	E	L	M	K	O	A	V	A	L	O
N	I	P	Q	A	B	U	C	I	A	U
R	A	S	B	E	N	F	T	C	N	N
O	T	A	H	I	T	I	J	A	D	D
B	A	L	I	A	T	L	A	M	I	L
R	O	C	R	E	T	E	V	F	O	A
Y	A	I	N	I	D	R	A	S	Y	N
I	P	S	T	Y	L	I	C	I	S	D

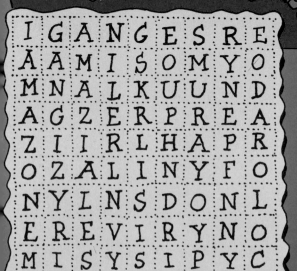

16 ▷ Waterways

The map (above) also shows seven famous rivers of the world. See if you can find their names in the word puzzle at left.

I	G	A	N	G	E	S	R	E
A	A	M	I	S	O	M	Y	O
M	N	A	L	K	U	U	N	D
A	G	Z	E	R	P	R	E	A
Z	I	I	R	L	H	A	P	R
O	Z	A	L	I	N	Y	F	O
N	Y	L	N	S	D	O	N	L
E	R	E	V	I	R	Y	N	O
M	I	S	Y	S	I	P	Y	C

Spare room search

For years everybody has dumped so much stuff in Granny's spare room that things are very hard to find. Each of the four searchers know in their minds what they are looking for, but they need your help to find each object!

19 Stargaze maze

Make your way from top to bottom – in less than one minute!

20 Ship shapes

Look closely at the tanker and the sails of the sailing ship and you should be able to see what countries they have come from. (Clue: it may help to look at the page from different angles.)

21 Muddled move

Lady Ashburton-Biddlewig is moving house, and has hired two movers to do the job. Her new address is 6 Oak Drive. Finally the men think they have finished the job. *Have all the items arrived safely at the correct address? Let's hope nothing is broken!*

22 Problematic ports

Which port should our brave explorer trust to lead him to the middle of South America?

Caracas

Belem

Guayaquil

Lima

23 Double jigsaw trouble

By transferring the jumbled lines in the left-hand grids to the correct place in the right-hand grids (using the grid references), you should be able to form two pictures.
(Clue: both illustrations are of South American animals.)

Rio de Janeiro

Santiago

Buenos Aires

5B	3D	4B	3A	1D
2A	5D	5A / 1C		3C
5C	1B	4D	4C	3B
1A	2D	2C	2B	4A

	1	2	3	4	5
A					
B					
C					
D					

5D	5A	4B	2D	1D
5B	4D	4C / 3B		2B
2C	3C	4A	1B	3D
1A	5C	1C	3A	2A

	1	2	3	4	5
A					
B					
C					
D					

26

```
S E I R R E H C R P L
T B A N A N A S L O E
R L E Q U E P E A R S
A N P S L T P L U M S
W S N O M E L O M G E
B N S G N O E G U R H
E G R A P E S N T A C
R L T S T O C I R P A
R E R S E G N A R O E
I M A N G O S F C S P
E W A T E R M E L O N
S E N I R E G N A T O
```

◆ 24 Fruit salad

The names of all the fruits in the picture are hidden in the word puzzle. As usual, the words may run in any direction!

◆ 25 Fishy finish

How long will it take you to finish up in the fish's stomach, by the shortest route? It shouldn't take you more than thirty seconds!

Alien adventure

By looking at Xenfo's wonderful collection of souvenirs, you should be able to list the places he visited on Earth.

The Solutions

Absent-minded artist
These are the three missing shapes.

Baffling butterflies
The butterflies at the top and the bottom are not symmetrical.

Southern stars

Strings attached
The boy's name is Tom, and the dinosaur is a *psittacosaurus*, which means "parrot-faced lizard." And it's true – there *was* such an animal.

5 **Royal reflection**

 Mind-twisting mass
The bridge will easily carry the dinosaur. It weighs 29.5 tons, including the boy's weight.

 African safari
Lagos is the correct harbor for our explorer to enter.

Double vision

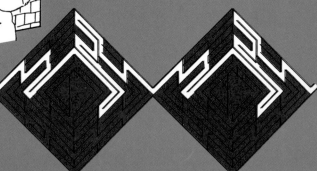

 6 **Country connection**
The country is New Zealand.

 7 **Around in circles**
The four animals are elephant, aardvark, mongoose, and platypus.

 12 **El Rancho Labyrinto**
The correct sequence of answers is: Paris, spiders, composer, the wind, marks, stars, yellow, in Korea, 212°F, Batavia, 1066 AD, hissing, I've found

 8 **Big Dipper baffler**

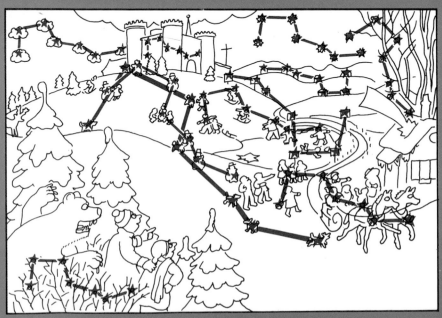

13 Aussie odyssey

Our intrepid explorer should start his trek from Darwin.

14 Blowing in the wind

The answer blowing in the wind is that the yacht at the SE point matches the one in the middle.

15 Island hopping

The seventeen islands are:

1. Bali
2. Borneo
3. Corsica
4. Crete
5. Cuba
6. Cyprus
7. Honshu
8. Ireland
9. Jamaica
10. Java
11. Madagascar
12. Malta
13. Newfoundland
14. Sardinia
15. Sicily
16. Tahiti
17. Tasmania

16 Waterways

The seven rivers are:

1. Amazon
2. Colorado
3. Don
4. Ganges
5. Murray
6. Nile
7. Rhine

17 Dangerous district

If our anonymous caller looked more closely, he may have noticed these serious crimes and silly mistakes being committed outside his window:

1. Two men are fishing from the bridge.
2. The boat is breaking the speed limit.
3. The blue car is going through a red light.
4. The tow rope between the boat and the car is incorrectly attached.
5. Children are in the boat being towed.
6. A woman is being robbed at gun point!
7. A boy is playing hopscotch in the middle of the road.
8. Workmen are lifting a piano through a window without warning pedestrians.
9. Someone has left a skateboard at the bottom of the stairs.
10. Children are balancing on the wall.
11. The pizza-maker is smoking while preparing food.
12. Children are playing on the railway line.
13. A cat is on the counter of a place serving food.
14. Camping is not allowed in the public park.
15. Posters have been stuck on the wall.
16. Someone is dropping a banana skin on the ground.
17. Flying kites near power lines is not permitted!
18. A car is going the wrong way around the traffic circle.
19. It is forbidden to ride a bicycle without holding the handlebars.
20. A robber is stealing from a woman's handbag.
21. A dog is digging up a flower bed.
22. Drinking while driving is definitely illegal!
23. A boy just threw a ball through a shop window.
24. A dog is sitting in a cafe where dogs are not allowed.
25. A man in the cafe is sitting with his feet on the table.
26. A woman is emptying a bucket into the street.
27. Finally, it *must* be illegal to keep seven kangaroos in a tiny cage on a rooftop!

Spare room search

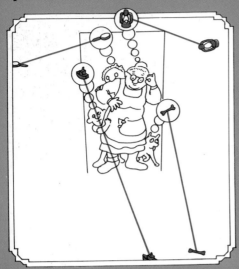

 Stargaze maze

 Ship shapes
The sailing ship comes from the U.S.A. and the cargo comes from Taiwan. If you can't work this one out, look at the page from an angle to recognize the elongated letters.

Muddled move

They broke the table. <u>And</u> my frog!
<u>And</u> they lost my little Eiffel Tower <u>altogether</u>!
And on top of it all - it <u>was</u> the wrong address!

 Problematic ports
Buenos Aires is the correct port.

 **Double jigsaw trouble**

Llama

Armadillo

 Fruit salad
The thirteen fruits are:

Apples	Mangos	Plums
Bananas	Oranges	Strawberries
Cherries	Peaches	Tangerines
Grapes	Pears	Watermelon
Lemons		

Fishy finish

 Alien adventure
Xenfo visited, starting from top left,

Athens, Greece (Parthenon); Moscow, Russia (St Basil's Cathedral); San Francisco, USA (Golden Gate Bridge); Sydney, Australia (Opera House); London, England (Big Ben and Bowler Hat); Paris, France (Eiffel Tower); Berlin, Germany (Brandenburg Gate); New York, USA (Statue of Liberty); Agra, India (Taj Mahal); Pisa, Italy (Leaning Tower); and Beijing, China (Ch'i Nien Tien).